SIMON
FRASER

AINSLIE MANSON

CANADIAN PATHFINDERS SERIES

Grolier Limited
TORONTO

Cover Illustration: Colin Gillies

Maps: Michele Nidenoff, pages 12, 18, 25, 38

Photo credits: Provincial Archives of British Columbia, page 4; Public Archives of Canada, pages 8 (C2001), 10 (C164), 16 (C167), 17 (C3610), 20 (C118263), 21 (C2772), 29 (C70270), 35 (C6641), 38, 40 (C1346); Hudson's Bay Company Archives/Public Archives of Manitoba, pages 22 and 45; Media Services, Manitoba Department of Education, page 26.

Canadian Cataloguing in Publication Data

Manson, Ainslie
  Simon Fraser

(Canadian pathfinder series)
ISBN 0-7172-2569-0

1. Fraser, Simon, 1776-1862 - Juvenile literature.
2. Northwest, Canadian - Discovery and exploration - Juvenile literature.
3. Canada - Exploring expeditions - Juvenile literature.
4. North West Company - Biography - Juvenile literature.
5. Explorers - Canada - Biography - Juvenile literature.
6. Fur traders - Canada - Biography - Juvenile literature.
I. Title.   II. Series.

FC3212.1.F7M3 1990   971.2'01'092   C90-095090-0
F1060.7.F7M3 1990

123456789   DWF   987654321

Printed and Bound in Canada

Contents

"I have been for a long period among the Rocky Mountains, but have never seen anything to equal this country, for I cannot find words to describe our situation at times. We had to pass where no human being should venture."

Excerpt from Simon Fraser's journal, June 26, 1808.

The Early Years

Simon Fraser was born at a turbulent time in North American history. In 1775, the year before his birth, the first shots in the American Revolution were fired. At that time, his parents, Simon and Isabella (Grant) Fraser, were living near Bennington, in what is now the state of Vermont. They had emigrated from Scotland only two years earlier.

The Frasers had a large family; Simon was their ninth child. They had immigrated because they felt America would provide opportunities for a better life. Although they had cousins in the American colonies and in Canada, they still missed their highland home. The three years before Simon's birth were lonely and confusing for them.

They had lived briefly in Albany, New York, before moving north and settling near Bennington. Hugh Fraser, one of their many cousins, had lived in this area for several years. They sensed that Hugh was not well liked by his neighbours, but they felt that whatever his quarrel was, it had nothing to do with them.

The Frasers went ahead and bought a farm with 160 acres (65 ha) of land and a modest but comfortable farmhouse. They worked hard on the land and by the time Simon was born, they had increased the cleared portion from 112 to 124 acres (45 to 50 ha). They had three yoke of oxen, two horses, a colt and twenty-four sheep, and were beginning to feel reasonably confident about the future of their farm.

Shattered Dreams

The Fraser's feelings of security were short-lived.

They became entangled in a dispute over the title of their property. New state boundaries were outlined, and they lost about half of their best land.

They were still reeling from this blow when the conflict between Britain and its rebellious American colonies reached the point of no return. In 1776, the year Simon was born, the thirteen colonies declared their independence. Britain immediately began an all-out effort to crush the revolution's progress.

Not everyone who lived in the thirteen colonies was in favour of independence. Thousands, including Simon's parents, chose to remain loyal to Britain. Unfortunately for the Fraser family, the citizens of Bennington were almost all rebels. Simon's father had been secretly working for the Loyalist cause ever since the first signs of unrest. Now his actions became public knowledge, and the whole family was shunned. Their cousin Hugh was a Loyalist too, but he soon fled to the New York area, which was in British hands. The Frasers felt very much alone in their allegiance.

Simon was still a baby when his father and his eldest brother, William, joined the British forces in 1777. He was too young to be aware of his mother's anguish and her loneliness when her rebel relations would no longer speak to her.

Simon's father moved up the ranks quickly and became a captain. He fought in the Battle of Bennington, a major battle that took place just a few kilometres from the Fraser farm. He was captured and taken to a jail in Albany.

Simon never saw his father again. Conditions were grim for the prisoners, and Captain Fraser became seriously ill. His family pleaded to have him released. They gathered names on a petition, but no one would listen to their case.

Simon was not yet three when his father died after thirteen months in prison. The little boy did not really remember his father, but he was now old enough to be aware of the grief and tension in his home.

Isabella Fraser's American cousins came to visit, but not to offer their help or consolation. They came only to try to persuade Angus, the second son, to join the rebels. Life would have been a little less lonely for the family had he agreed, but he refused again and again. With each refusal, the family was made to pay a fine. Their farmhouse was vandalized. Many of their possessions were stolen. More were confiscated. One by one their animals had to be sold to make ends meet.

Peace and a New Start
The last battle of the American Revolution was fought in October 1781. It was a decisive victory for the rebels, and in 1783 the Treaty of Paris recognized the United States as an independent country.

By this time, Simon was seven. His brother William had gone to Canada during the war and had remained there. Since peace did not put an end to the mistreatment of Loyalists, his mother decided that the rest of the family should go to Canada as well. Angus was sent north to make arrangements for the move. He went to Montreal where his father's brother John had become a judge. John Fraser kindly offered financial support.

The Frasers were fortunate to be able to settle immediately in an established community. Many Loyalists spent months in camps like this one near present-day Kingston, waiting for the government to assign them land.

The Frasers sold what they had left and joined the long lines of Loyalists moving northward to live under the British Crown. They first settled in the small village of Coteau du Lac, on the St. Lawrence River, above the city of Montreal. Loyalists had been settling in this area since the early years of the war, and the Frasers found it reassuring to see the progress they had made.

William and Angus, many years older than Simon, soon settled on farms of their own. They acquired land grants of 200 acres (80 ha) each at St. Andrews near Cornwall, on the Upper St. Lawrence. Eventually Mrs. Fraser and the younger children also moved to the Cornwall area.

A Time of Growth

Little is known about Simon's first few years in Canada, but life was not easy for the Frasers. The Loyalist families all had to work hard to establish farms and communities in the heavily wooded lands along the Upper St. Lawrence. All family members, including children Simon's age, were expected to do their share.

Simon's father had been a well-educated man, with a taste for poetry and music, and Isabella Fraser undoubtedly would have liked a good education for her children. She would almost certainly have made sure that they learned to read and write. But at that time there were no schools for the Loyalist children to attend, and she would not have been able to afford to send them away to boarding school. She must therefore have been pleased when Judge John Fraser offered, in 1790, to bring Simon to Montreal for some formal education.

Judge Fraser lived in a large stone house in the old part of the city and was a highly respected citizen. Simon enjoyed the comfort of his uncle's house and was fascinated by the bustling, growing city of Montreal. It was quite unlike any place he had ever been before, and he eagerly explored its narrow cobbled streets. He particularly enjoyed walking along the shore, watching as goods were carried back and forth from the great sailing ships in the little flat-bottomed *bateaux*.

At this time, Simon does not seem to have been very enthusiastic about book-learning. He was a quiet boy, with few close friends. He took life seriously, and his sometimes blank, stern expression was frequently interpreted as sullen. It was more a look of concentration, however. He watched and listened constantly, and this is how he learned best.

Few boys continued their studies after the age of sixteen and Simon was no exception. He soon realized that much of the activity that so intrigued him in Montreal was centred on the fur trade. Just about everyone he met, including two of his mother's brothers, seemed to be associated in some way with this fascinating industry. Simon asked his uncles, Peter and Donald Grant, many questions and never tired of listening to them tell of their experiences. He longed to become involved himself.

Another rather awe-inspiring family connection, on his father's side of the family, was Simon McTavish. A well-known figure in the city, McTavish had initiated the idea of the North West Company, the organization that dominated the fur trade in Montreal.

Simon McTavish

The Apprenticeship Years

Simon observed that McTavish's own small company, McTavish, Frobisher & Co., dominated the North West Company and made most of the decisions for the ever-expanding organization. McTavish was something of a tyrant, but he never forgot his friends and his family as his power increased. He had hired three of his nephews to article as clerks, and in 1792, he took Simon on as well.

These boys may have been hired thanks to their powerful relation, but there were no shortcuts for them once they were in the door. In the North West Company, merit alone counted. No matter how rich or poor, how socially acceptable or powerless an

employee might be, promotion was assured only if he possessed and displayed ability.

A clerk in the fur trade was simply an assistant. He went wherever he was needed and did what he was told to do. Usually he started at the bottom of the ladder, in the warehouse. He loaded and unloaded furs, packed and stacked furs, counted, carried and carted furs.

Simon's round face with the set, determined chin often wore a weary, grim expression during those first months of his apprenticeship, but he never refused a task that was tossed his way. His shoulders grew broad and his back grew strong. Even when he was inactive, the grey-blue eyes

View of Montreal. For all its importance as a shipping centre, Montreal still had no wharves or proper landing facilities in the 1790s.

The North West Company

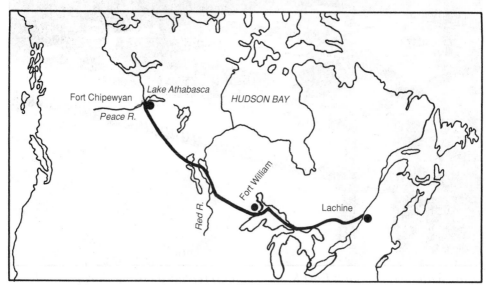

This map shows the voyageurs' route from Lachine, near Montreal, to the Athabasca country. Each stage of the long journey — Lachine–Fort William and Fort William–Fort Chipewyan — took about six weeks.

The North West Company was not a true company but more like an umbrella organization for a number of small fur trading companies. It was formed in the late 1770s by a group of Montreal fur traders who had finally realized the folly of competing with one another as well as with their giant rival, the Hudson's Bay Company.

Once they had joined forces, the Nor'Westers quickly built up a very efficient organization. There were two types of partners: the Montreal partners, who were responsible for marketing the furs and providing essential trade goods and supplies;

and the wintering partners, who stayed in the West to look after the forts and trade with the Natives. There were also many employees, including clerks and guides and, of course, the famous *voyageurs*, who paddled the canoes.

The distances the Nor'Westers had to cover were enormous — 6000 kilometres, for instance, from Montreal to the fur-rich Athabasca country. There was no way the round trip could be made in one season. The Nor'Westers came up with a neat solution to this problem.

Every spring, brigades of freight canoes, loaded with supplies and

Fort William (originally Fort Kaministiquia) replaced Grand Portage as the company's western headquarters in 1803. It is seen here as reconstructed about 15 km from the original site at Thunder Bay.

trade goods, left Montreal for the company's large supply depot at Grand Portage, at the head of Lake Superior. Meanwhile, smaller *canots du nord* laden with furs were heading in from the company's far-flung trading posts in what was called the *pays d'en haut*.

The two groups stayed about a month at Grand Portage. The Montreal and wintering partners who had been able to come discussed business and socialized, the canoe crews rested up, and clerks sorted and repacked furs and supplies. Then the wintering partners set off for their remote posts with their provisions and trade goods, and the Montrealers

returned home with their loads of furs.

This system worked well, but it was very expensive, and costs were a constant worry to the North West Company partners. In this respect, the Hudson's Bay company enjoyed a considerable advantage: they could transport goods much more cheaply by sea to their posts on Hudson Bay, right in the middle of the continent.

The further the Nor'Westers pushed into the rich fur country beyond Lake Athabasca, the more expensive their system became. It was the search for cheaper and/or shorter supply routes that prompted the many journeys of exploration that the Nor'Westers undertook.

Fort Chipewyan, on Lake Athabasca, where Simon Fraser served for a time during his early years in the pays d'en haut.

under the tousled reddish hair were intent. Simon was practising his old skill of learning by watching and listening.

His ability was soon recognized and within a few years he was given the opportunity to continue his apprenticeship in the Athabasca region of the *pays d'en haut*.

Fraser now found he had a whole new set of skills to master. As a clerk he would not normally be expected to paddle and repair his own canoe, but to survive in the wilderness he had to know how. He also had to learn to snowshoe, repair his snowshoes, hunt and interpret signs of a change in the weather.

Life in a remote post was lonely and difficult. Most posts were uncomfortable and the diet was monotonous. Winter was bitterly cold; spring and summer were made miserable by thick clouds of black flies and mosquitoes. The work was often back-breaking, sometimes dangerous, and there were spells, especially in winter, of total, mind-numbing boredom.

Fraser proved himself an excellent trader and an able leader. He had great stamina, determination and courage. He was physically very strong and though he was not tall, this was probably an advantage, as shorter men fitted more comfortably into heavily loaded canoes.

When the North West Company partners met at Grand Portage in late June 1801, it was unanimously resolved that Fraser and five others "should be admitted Partners of the North West Company for one Forty sixth share each, their Interest in the same to Commence with the Outfit of the Year 1802..."

A partnership at the age of twenty-five was a great achievement for Fraser. Wintering partners had enormous responsibility both for the profits of the company and for the lives and well-being of their employees. Partnership was rarely granted to anyone under the age of thirty. Simon Fraser had demonstrated exceptional ability.

Go West, Young Man

After Simon McTavish died in 1804, his nephew William McGillivray was made Chief Director of the reorganized North West Company. McGillivray summoned Simon Fraser to the annual general meeting at Fort Kaministiquia in the summer of 1805. (The company's western headquarters had been moved because the border established between Canada and the United States had put Grand Portage on the American side.)

The partners had a lot to discuss that year. McTavish had been against expanding operations west of the Rocky Mountains, but now the time had come. The partners were eager not only to secure more furs but also to resume the search for a trade route from the Athabasca country to the Pacific.

Alexander Mackenzie had reached the Pacific in 1793, but by an overland route that was useless for trade purposes. McGillivray now appointed Fraser to take charge of operations beyond the Rockies. He was to establish contact with the Natives, build trading posts and explore the full length of the river that had defeated Mackenzie. This was the river that today bears Fraser's name, but it was then thought to be the Columbia.

Fraser left for Fort Chipewyan as soon as he could. He had a lot of planning and organizing to do before he could carry out his mission.

William McGillivray

Rocky Mountain Portage

In the autumn of 1805, Fraser set out along the Peace River with a party of about twenty-five men, including two excellent clerks, John Stuart and James McDougall. When they reached the lower end of the Peace River Canyon, they chose a site for their first post, Rocky Mountain Portage. This was to be the supply base for the chain of posts they hoped to build beyond the mountains.

Fraser left John Stuart in charge of construction. Then, with McDougall and a few of the other men, he headed west to explore the territory a little, before winter set in. As Alexander Mackenzie had done twelve years earlier, Fraser and his party followed the Peace and then took its southern fork, the Parsnip. Two days up the Parsnip,

Furs and trade goods were packed in compact bundles called pièces. Each one weighed about 40 kg, and a voyageur was expected to carry two. One was placed in a sling supported by a wide strap around the forehead. Then the other was set on top of the first.

17

they discovered a smaller river (the Pack), which Mackenzie had failed to mention in his journals.

Fort McLeod

The river brought them to a small lake that teemed with trout. After weeks of pemmican, fish was such a treat that they called the lake Trout Lake. (It was later renamed McLeod Lake.)

The Sekani Natives who lived in this area were friendly and kind, and this therefore seemed an ideal location for a second post. Fraser and his men cut trees and constructed a crude log cabin. It would be the first house in the first permanent non-Native settlement in what is now the Province of British

Fraser named the area west of the Rockies New Caledonia, probably because it reminded him of his mother's descriptions of her homeland. (Caledonia was the ancient Roman name for the Scottish Highlands.)

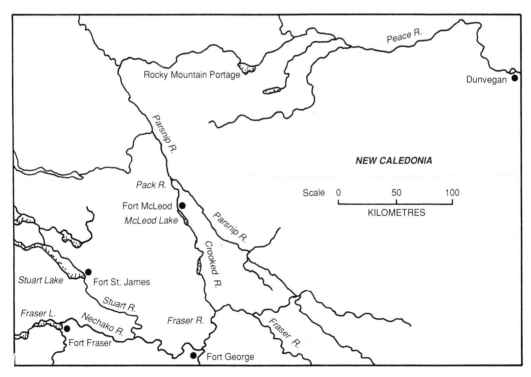

Columbia. Fraser called it Trout Lake Post, but its name was later changed to Fort McLeod.

By the time the essential work was done, temperatures were dropping and snow was beginning to fall. Leaving three men to winter at the new post, Fraser set off to return to his base camp by snowshoe.

The Long Winter

At Christmas time, Simon Fraser and James McDougall hiked about 300 kilometres back along the Peace River to Fort Dunvegan. Dunvegan was a new post, which over the next few years would become very important to the North West Company. A number of women and children would come to live there, making it seem much more homelike than many of the more remote posts. A renowned kitchen garden ensured that there was never a scarcity of food. The men liked visiting Dunvegan. The fort had an excellent library and they claimed that here they could nourish not only their bodies, but their minds as well.

Archibald Norman McLeod, Fraser's fellow partner in the North West Company, was also at Dunvegan for Christmas 1805. Possibly Fraser's main reason for making the trip was to consult with him and discuss his progress, problems and plans for the journey to the Pacific that he hoped to manage the following summer.

Back at Rocky Mountain Portage, Fraser, who was never a man to sit idle, kept his men busy. When construction of the buildings was completed, he put them to work carrying and dragging great

Mackenzie first tried to find a route to the Pacific Ocean in 1789 but reached the Arctic Ocean instead. He tried again in 1793 and this time he succeeded. He travelled only a short way down the Fraser, however, before turning westward and completing his journey overland.

loads of equipment and trade goods overland to the upper end of the canyon. That way, everything would be there, ready to load into canoes, as soon as the rivers were free of ice.

The Natives of the region brought their furs to the fort and traded them for food, wool blankets, iron goods, lengths of material and some clothing. Fraser encouraged them to return with more furs and to spread the word about his new post to others. With his plans for future posts and his trip to the Pacific in mind, he also questioned them about the unknown land beyond the mountains. He was distressed to learn that the Carrier Natives, who lived a little to the west, were obtaining American goods from the coast, but he hoped that his chain of forts would eventually prevent this trafficking.

Meanwhile, trouble had developed at Fort McLeod and the post had been abandoned. James McDougall was sent to investigate, and once he had things straightened out, he did a little advance exploration. Travelling three and a half days on snowshoes, he reached a lake his Native guide called Nakazleh (later Stuart Lake).

McDougall was enchanted by Stuart Lake and recommended it as the ideal location for a third post. It was very large (360 km²) and he found that one of its outlets eventually led to the Fraser River, which they still believed to be the Columbia.

The 1806 Exploration

Break-up on the Peace was late that year, and Fraser had to abandon his plan to follow the Fraser River to the coast. There simply would not be time to make

the round trip. Instead he decided to explore the water route to Stuart Lake and organize the building of a fort there. Then he would return to the Fraser River and go down it at least as far as Mackenzie had in 1793.

Even this, however, was not to be. Just about everything that could go wrong on an expedition of this kind did go wrong. The canoes Fraser and his party set out in were in very bad shape. The men had to stop constantly and repair them. Eventually they had to replace them entirely, and this held them up at Fort McLeod for two and a half weeks. The crewmen were not very skilled, and to make matters worse, one or another was always getting sick, causing further delays. The party finally made it to Stuart Lake on July 26, more than two months after they set out. Fraser described it in his journal

Even the best birchbark canoes needed frequent repairs. Those in which Fraser set out in 1806 were far from the best, and he and his men seem to have spent almost as much time on shore repairing them as they did travelling.

as a "fine, large lake" and set the men to building his third post — the future Fort St. James.

The area proved to have its problems, however. Though it had seemed to McDougall like a land of plenty, the men were starving. The salmon run was late and even game and berries were scarce. The Natives were short of food themselves and were therefore not enthusiastic about sharing.

It was too late in the season now to undertake even a partial exploration of the Fraser River. Besides, none of the men had the strength for such a trip. They were growing listless and irritable from lack of nourishing food.

The Natives guided them to a lake sixty-five kilometres to the south. It was a long haul on empty stomachs, but it proved to be a worthwhile journey. Fish and game were plentiful. There were several villages in the vicinity and the Natives seemed eager to trade. Fraser built his fourth post, later called Fort Fraser, at this location.

John Stuart, in later years.

More Waiting

That winter (1806-7) Fraser's new posts all did a brisk trade in the richest, silkiest beaver Fraser had ever seen. The only handicap was the long carrying distance back across the country to Montreal. It was more important than ever to find a new trade route to the Pacific coast. But to Fraser's great disappointment, the supplies and trade goods he needed for the trip had not arrived in 1806. He would have to wait another year.

When the beaver pelts went east in the early spring of 1807, Fraser included urgent requests for more supplies and reinforcements. At the end of the summer Jules Maurice Quesnel and Hugh Faries arrived with two loaded canoes. They were given a warm reception. A few of the long-awaited supplies made up the festive feast that night, but most were saved for the expedition.

It was months since Fraser and his men had had news from home. After dinner they plied their visitors with questions. Fraser was interested to hear that Fort Kaministiquia had been renamed Fort William in honour of William McGillivray. More directly important to him was the information that efforts to obtain transit rights through Hudson Bay had failed. As a result, instructions from Fort William were explicit...a new trade route *must* be found.

News from below the border was also alarming. An American expedition led by Lewis and Clark had just returned east after a successful trip across the continent. They had travelled down the lower part of the Columbia River to the Pacific Ocean.

The news was distressing because no borders had yet been finalized in this western part of the continent. The Nor'Westers feared that the Americans might lay claim to the great spread of land south and west of their forts. Exploring that land was now more important than ever.

In the autumn of 1807, Fraser built his fifth and final post, Fort George, at the junction of the Nechako River and the Fraser. It would serve both as a trading post and as a base from which they could set off down the river as early as possible in the spring. They could afford no further delays.

Where No Human Being Should Venture

Leaving Hugh Faries in charge of the post, Fraser and his party pushed off from the shores at Fort George in the grey, early morning light of May 28, 1808. The men cheered, and from the stern of his canoe, Simon Fraser looked back and watched the figure of Hugh Faries growing smaller. The strong current drew them quickly downstream and out of sight of the fort.

Fraser was proud and sure of the men he had hand-picked for this journey of exploration. They were all young, strong and full of enthusiasm. At age thirty-two, he was the old man of the group.

John Stuart, his second in command, was twenty-nine. Simon Fraser had great respect for Stuart, one of the few men he considered a true friend. Jules Quesnel, his other clerk, was always cheerful and agreeable. Twenty-two-year-old Quesnel claimed he had learned at an early age to get along with everyone...growing up in a family of thirteen children.

There were nineteen voyageurs on the expedition and two Carrier guides. Six men rode in each of the four birchbark canoes. They experienced several sizable rapids (a preview of what lay ahead) even before they stopped for breakfast at eleven, six hours after setting out.

The river was high and overflowing its banks in spring-time flood. It was the most dangerous time of the year on the Fraser, but the men did not know that. As they sped along with the swift current, Fraser noted with interest the Natives' summer residences along the shore. He was charmed by the open rolling hills. He would not be charmed for long.

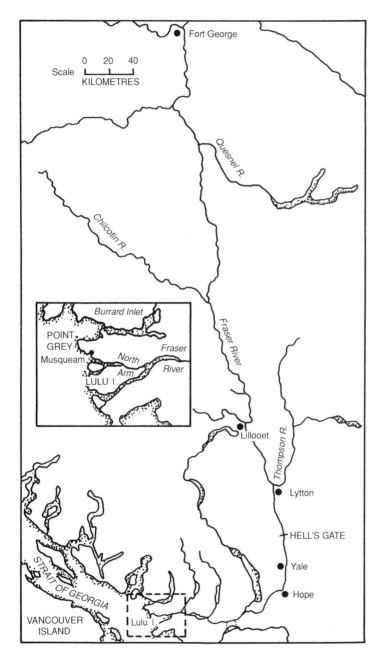

The Fraser River.

Several times during the day, voyageurs stopped, lit up their pipes and enjoyed a short rest. This routine was so common and so regular that distances came to be measured in "pipes." The average distance between rest stops was 7 or 8 km.

Valuable Assistance

The first Natives they met suggested that the explorers should remain with them until the next tribe along the route could be warned of their coming. A sudden appearance might cause alarm. It seemed wise advice.

Fraser was told again and again that the river was impassable and that if he wanted to travel to the sea, he should travel overland. But Fraser felt he had to follow the river in order to determine the extent of its hazards and to carry out an honest survey. He also wondered if perhaps the Natives, who were very poor, were trying to dissuade him because they wished his party to stay and trade with them. He soon learned that they were telling the truth.

The river grew worse. On June 1, they reached a narrow three-kilometre stretch that was wild with whirlpools and rapids. Sheer cliffs rose straight up on either side and Fraser felt they had no choice but to paddle on. He realized his mistake immediately when he sent his five best canoeists on a trial run. They flew from one danger to another until the canoe was finally hurled against a low rock that jutted out from the bank. The men managed to catch hold of the rock, saving themselves and their canoe from certain destruction.

As the five men clung desperately to the rock, Fraser and the others set about rescuing them. They had to ease themselves down the vertical bank, plunging daggers into cracks to keep themselves from sliding down into the river. It took the rest of the day to cut steps into the rock and raise the men and canoe to safety.

On the long, perilous portage that followed, one of the voyageurs somehow got his pack wedged between two rocks. He was pinned to the cliff's edge, unable to move either forward or back. Fraser crawled to his aid and had to sacrifice the pack to free him. They thanked God that the pack was not a man as they watched it bounce down, down over the precipice and into the churning water below.

The Natives Fraser encountered along this stretch of the river had horses, and they kindly offered their help to carry the packs over the long portage. The canoes were almost impossible to manoeuvre along the steep narrow trail. Reluctantly, Fraser decided to leave two of them behind.

This meant that once they were able to travel by

water again, the men had to take turns walking. The canoes needed constant repair as birchbark was torn and sterns ripped off, and the men found their feet needed constant repair too. They were blistered and full of thorns, and a pair of moccasins lasted no more than a day. Though riding in the canoe was often harrowing, at least it was easier on the feet.

Fortunately, most of the Natives were friendly, helpful and eager to trade. Before too long, Fraser was able to obtain two much needed canoes.

No Turning Back

The river's perils were continuous, and often the steep banks allowed no escape. At one point high cliffs on either side leaned in toward each other, seeming almost to meet at the top. The paddlers could only pray as they shot through the tunnel-like narrows. When they reached calmer water, they gazed back in wonder, and waited for their hearts to stop pounding.

Although he did not know it, Fraser was now halfway to his destination. The river was obviously not navigable, but he never considered turning back. He would not turn westward and travel overland, either. He had been given instructions to follow the river, and follow it he would.

For his men Fraser kept a stiff upper lip, but in his journal, in the privacy of his tent, he wrote: "I scarcely ever saw anything so dreary and seldom so dangerous in any country; and at present while I am writing this, whatever way I turn, mountains upon mountains, whose summits are covered with eternal snows, close the gloomy scene."

"Our situation was really dangerous," Fraser wrote on June 5, *"being constantly between steep and high banks where there was no possibility of stopping the canoe."*

Two weeks after setting out, the explorers reached a point beyond which they could not continue by water. They had to cache their canoes and as much of their baggage as they could do without until the return journey. They carried on, as close to the river as possible.

Fraser found it difficult to keep up his men's

" . . . where no human being should venture."

morale. He felt extremely insecure himself: "Here we are, in a strange Country, surrounded by dangers, and difficulties.... Our situation is critical and highly unpleasant." He would not admit defeat however: "We shall endeavour to make the best of it: what cannot be cured, must be endured."

At the junction of the Thompson River (Fraser named it after his fellow Nor'Wester David Thompson), the men were able to take to the water again. They borrowed canoes and also acquired extra guides. They were especially grateful to one kind chief and a young Native Fraser called The Little Fellow who offered to accompany them. Fraser listened to all their tales of what lay ahead but could not really believe that conditions could get any worse. They could, however. The party was about to reach the narrow gorge known today as Hell's Gate in the awesome Fraser Canyon .

Hell's Gate

Fraser was amazed, when in this treacherous spot, they were guided along a regular footpath indented in the rocks by constant use. The Native guides helpfully carted extra baggage and trotted along with no fear or difficulty. The terrified explorers walked sideways and dared not look down. The roar of the river was deafening. They could feel its thunderous power vibrating through their bodies as they clung to the rockface.

In several places ladders made from branches joined by vines and strips of hide stretched, swinging, up toward the sky, then down toward the river. The men repeatedly had to climb up and down them as there was no other way to get around great jutting boulders that blocked the way. They felt like spiders clinging to a swaying web.

It was a nightmare, but like all bad dreams it finally came to an end. Incredibly, everyone made it safely through.

A couple of days later, they met a coastal tribe for the first time and were treated very kindly. Invited to a feast, they were seated on neat woven mats and served delicious roasted salmon in attractive wooden dishes. The Natives on this side of the mountains had few dealings with the interior Natives. Their language, manners and customs were completely different. Their homes too were different from any Fraser had yet seen. They were made from overlapping planks 8 to 10 centimetres thick, and they were enormous, sometimes almost 200 metres long and 20 metres wide. One of these buildings often housed a whole tribe.

Fraser was fascinated by the huge nets that they used for catching deer and other large animals. He also admired their rugs, which were made from the wool of wild goat and dog's hair. The dogs were specially bred for their hair and shorn like sheep.

Fraser was warned that the Cowichan people he would meet nearer the coast were very aggressive. He was not about to let that stop him. His men paddled on, relieved to have finally reached more peaceful water. Now the canoes they borrowed were hollowed out from enormous cedar trees. They moved from tribe to tribe, village to village, borrowing new canoes as they went.

As they got closer to the sea, the Natives they

met did indeed tend to be more hostile. A few of Fraser's men were so frightened they were reluctant to continue. Fraser urged them on.

Where The River Meets The Sea

As they neared the river delta, local Natives paddled out to greet them and volunteered one of their men as a guide to show them the correct channel to the sea. Fraser accepted, but he soon wondered if he had made a mistake. As the guide's companions followed, they became noisy and threatening. They were armed with bows and arrows, clubs and spears, and they sang a war song as they beat time with their paddles upon the side of the canoes. Then the guide Fraser had taken on began to sing and leap about in the unsteady canoe. Fraser had to threaten him angrily before he would sit still.

At last they reached what Fraser called a "bay of the sea" (the Strait of Georgia), and thankfully landed safely at the village of Musqueam. Fraser was given a conducted tour of an incredible 500-metre-long fort. But when the tour was over, he was told that he and his men should leave immediately or they would be attacked.

Returning to the shore, they discovered that in addition to the canoes that had pursued them, many Natives had followed along the shore. They could not interpret the silent, watchful faces, and to make matters worse, the tide had gone out. Their heavy cedar canoe was beached. As they set about dragging it to the water, the Natives continued to approach from all directions brandishing clubs.

As soon as they reached deep enough water, Fraser and his men climbed into the canoe. By this time the threatening followers were closing in, but they stopped when Fraser made it clear that he would fire upon them if they did not keep their distance.

Fraser was still eager to explore the coast and reach the open sea. They continued on for a while, but soon realized that they would not be able to land as they had no provisions and no hope of getting any. Reluctantly they turned their bow upstream.

They reached the village where they had spent the previous night without further trouble and camped nearby. Despite his fears and worries, Fraser still hoped for another chance to reach the main ocean — but he soon had to face the fact that even these villagers were showing signs of hostility. It became apparent that the one short glimpse they had had of the Strait of Georgia was all they were going to get.

Natives from the coast reappeared and with their encouragement, the locals became more aggressive. Normally Fraser found that moving slowly and remaining utterly calm was vital to peaceful negotiations. But he now realized he would not even be heard in the uproar that had erupted. He therefore pretended to be in a violent passion. He spoke loudly, using wild gestures. The Natives were so astonished that they calmed down and peace was restored...for the time being.

Homeward Bound

The chief did not want them to leave with his canoe,

but Fraser had to insist, realizing that the safety of his men was at stake. He left the angry chief standing on the shore, clutching a new blanket which he had not felt was a fair trade.

They were followed and threatened all that day. Hungry and tired, the voyageurs paddled on through the long night, not even daring to stop to rest. Fraser felt the full depth of his disappointment as hour after hour he strained his eyes to penetrate the curtain of darkness. He had not stayed long at the coast, but he had managed to take observations and he now knew

The Native villages Fraser encountered near the coast would have been similar to this one, sketched some years earlier by John Webber, an artist who travelled with Captain James Cook .

the bitter truth. This despicable river was not the Columbia. The mouth of this river was a full three degrees of latitude further to the north.

They had travelled over 800 kilometres down a river that had proved unnavigable. They had faced hostile Natives and they were still in desperate danger. Fraser felt the weight of his responsibility. How far behind were his pursuers? Would he get his men safely back to Fort George?

Day after day they were pursued. Fraser could no longer find words to reassure his men. They took up a position of defence on the shore, but several of the terrified voyageurs wanted to escape inland. Fraser feared he had a mutiny on his hands.

After much heated debate, he convinced the men that they must remain together. They shook hands and took an oath: "I solemnly swear before Almighty God," each man declared, "that I shall sooner perish than forsake in distress any of our crew during the present voyage." In better spirits, they then dressed in their best clothes and laughing and singing, they pushed off from the shore. Their astonished pursuers watched in bewilderment, then turned their canoes back downstream. Fraser was dumfounded but immensely relieved.

The river was still treacherous and it was not easy paddling against the current, but from there on they met only kind and helpful Natives. It had taken 36 days to travel down the river from Fort George. Surprisingly, they made it back in one day less.

Frustration and Resignation

Simon Fraser was frustrated with the outcome of the expedition, but during a brief rest at Ford George he reminded himself that he had done what he had been asked to do. He had accomplished his mission quickly and efficiently and without loss of life or injury to any of his men.

He checked up on each of his posts, and then before the rivers froze, he made a trip to Fort Chipewyan to report his findings. He spent only one more winter in New Caledonia. In the spring of 1809 he left for the East, satisfied that the posts were now all flourishing.

The North West Company granted Fraser a year's leave — a well-earned rest after many years of hard work. He was then reassigned to the Mackenzie River District, part of the Athabasca Department. This assignment was apparently a promotion, as he was in charge of a very large territory.

He remained there three years. Then after another leave he found himself wishing he did not have to return to the hardships of being a wintering partner. He was thirty-nine now and he had a strong desire to settle down.

Fraser had another reason, as well, for wanting to get out of the fur trade. The North West Company and the Hudson's Bay Company were constantly at each other's throats. Fraser was quite capable of settling small disputes, but he did not wish to become involved in battles and bloodshed.

He visited friends and family in the Cornwall area during his second leave and began looking at land to purchase. He decided he wanted to spend the rest of his life in this pleasant location and it was with great reluctance that he returned to work.

Fraser left Montreal in the spring of 1815 with Alex Mackenzie, nephew of the explorer, Sir Alexander Mackenzie. They planned to travel together as far as the new Red River Colony. Without realizing it, Simon Fraser was heading into exactly the sort of confrontation he hated.

The Red River Colony

The planning and development of the new settlement at Red River had caused a good deal of upset in recent years. The colony had been founded three years earlier by Sir Thomas Douglas, the fifth Earl of Selkirk. Selkirk had acquired from the Hudson's Bay Company a vast grant of land that included the whole area drained by the Red and Assiniboine Rivers. On this broad expanse of prairie he planned to settle poor crofters — tenant farmers from the Highlands of Scotland who were being thrown off their land to make room for sheep farming.

The Nor'Westers were outraged. The land Selkirk had acquired straddled their long standing fur-trading highway. Settlement would seriously affect their security, their communications and their pemmican supply. Lord Selkirk was a kind, unselfish man who was truly concerned about the plight of the crofters. But the Nor'Westers knew beyond a doubt that Selkirk's settlement meant the beginning of the end for their company.

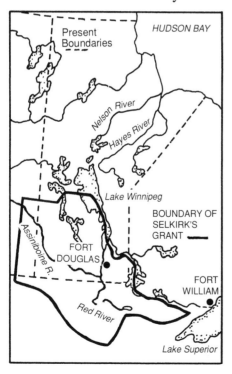

Lord Selkirk's grant.

Fraser knew little about the development of the Red River Colony. Paddling westward, Alex Mackenzie filled him in on the details he had missed.

The Métis, descendants of fur traders and Natives, were the only settlers in the area until the colonists arrived. They had their own way of life, based mainly on buffalo hunting. Not surprisingly, they considered the establishment of an agricultural settlement a danger to that way of life.

The settlers who arrived in 1812 lacked proper tools and equipment. The few crops they managed to plant were destroyed by grasshoppers, floods and early frosts, resulting in a desperate shortage of food. In a misguided attempt to resolve his problems, the colony's Governor, Miles Macdonell, passed an act known as "The Pemmican

The Red River Settlement in 1817, from a sketch believed to be by Lord Selkirk.

Proclamation." The act forbade the export of any pemmican from the area. The Nor'Westers considered the proclamation a declaration of war. For years they had obtained their pemmican supply from the Métis in this area for their Athabasca and far western traders.

When Macdonell went so far as to seize their pemmican supplies, they became determined to crush the settlement. To this end, they lured a hundred starving colonists away by offering them transportation and free land grants in Upper Canada. Meanwhile, they encouraged the Métis, who feared for their land and hunting rights, to terrorize the remaining settlers by burning crops and circling farmhouses firing their rifles.

About the time Fraser and Mackenzie appeared on the scene, the Nor'Westers had obtained a warrant for the Governor's arrest for seizing their pemmican. Macdonell surrendered in hopes that this would prevent any further harm to the settlers.

Although Fraser had not wanted to become involved in this dispute, he too believed that Miles Macdonell had gone too far. He and Mackenzie agreed to accompany the arrested Governor back to Fort William. When his mission was accomplished, Fraser met with William McGillivray and expressed his wish to resign. McGillivray pleaded with him not to desert the company at such a time of unrest. Fraser agreed to stay on for another year and returned one last time to Athabasca.

*Thomas Douglas,
Earl of Selkirk*

Seven Oaks
The situation at Red River did not improve. A new

Governor, Robert Semple, brought in more settlers, and an uneasy peace reigned for a while. Then in the spring of 1816, Semple heard that the Nor'Westers were planning more trouble. He responded by destroying their Red River post, Fort Gibraltar.

This was the final straw! Several Nor'Westers and a group of Métis rode on to Fort Douglas where Semple had his headquarters. They were met outside the fort, at a grove of trees known as Seven Oaks, by Semple and twenty-seven of his men. In the skirmish that followed, first the Governor was killed, then a Nor'Wester and twenty of Semple's men.

At the time, Lord Selkirk himself was en route to Red River, bringing a contingent of a hundred soldier-settlers. When he learned of the tragedy, he went instead to Fort William and vented his fury by arresting all the partners he found there. One of them was Simon Fraser who had come to attend the partners' meeting.

The arrested partners were sent under guard to Montreal. On the way they met with further disaster: a canoe capsized and nine men were drowned. The survivors were released on bail when they reached their destination. Two years later, Fraser went on trial along with his partners. They were all acquitted because of lack of evidence. Even before the trial Fraser had handed in his resignation. His fur trading days were over.

Fraser and His River In Later Years

Fraser settled near St. Andrews, in the township of Cornwall, where his two eldest brothers had taken land grants when the family first arrived in Canada.

He soon became an active, respected member of the community, involved in several different enterprises. He owned and managed a fair amount of farm land and had interests in a sawmill and a grist mill. The mills were helpful to the community but they were not very profitable.

Fraser was no longer a young man, and he was anxious to have a family of his own. He met and admired Catherine Macdonell of Matilda Township not far from Cornwall. They were married on June 7, 1820 when Fraser was forty-four years of age and Catherine was twenty-nine. They had nine children — five sons, three daughters, and another child who died in infancy.

Fraser was happy and content with family life. He had come to regret how little formal education he had and now spent much of his spare time reading. He was interested and well informed about everything that was going on in Canada and took a great interest in politics.

When rebellion broke out in both Upper and Lower Canada in 1837, Fraser was drawn into the action. He served as Captain with the 1st Regiment of the Stormont Militia. In November 1838, his regiment was called to support a force that was closing in on some rebels. Marching through the darkness, Fraser had a bad fall and seriously injured his right knee. It seemed such a ridiculous accident for a man who had braved without mishap the perils of the treacherous Fraser Canyon!

Fraser received a small pension as compensation for his injury, but from that time on he suffered a lot of pain. He found he could not carry on with his farm work or mill work. Repeatedly he applied to government departments and military medical boards for further financial aid. He had no success, and in his later years he and Catherine had a difficult time making ends meet.

Despite his problems, Fraser continued to enjoy visiting with four other North West Company partners who had settled in the area. He had become more sociable as he grew older, and these men became true, close friends. Their visits carried on for years, long after the North West Company had been absorbed by the Hudson's Bay Company.

On August 1, 1859, Fraser and John McDonald of Garth, the last of the old wintering partners, met for a final visit. They were in their eighties now, and McDonald was not well. They knew that they would not meet again. Realizing the significance of the occasion, they drew up a statement as a seal to their long friendship and a declaration of their beliefs:

We are the last of the N.W. Partners. We are both aged, we have lived in mutual esteem and friendship, we have done our duty in the stations alloted us without fear or reproach. We have braved many dangers, we have run many risks. We cannot accuse one another of any thing mean & dirty through life, nor [have we] done any disagreeable actions, nor wrong to others... We part as we have lived in sincere friendship & mutual good will.

Macdonald died within the year. Before Fraser died, he learned about the Gold Rush in British Columbia. Hundreds of prospectors were struggling up Fraser's river from the coast to search for gold in the Cariboo.

Fraser's Death

Simon Fraser died on August 11, 1862, after a very short illness. He was eighty-six. Catherine, his wife of forty years, died the following day before she had even been told of his death. They were buried in a single grave.

Fraser had been a respected citizen of Cornwall. His obituary in the *Cornwall Freeholder* read:

> *In Mr. Fraser the country loses not only one of its most respectable and honored residents, but one of the most illustrious men who ever settled within its borders. One of the few survivors of the fine old 'North Westers', Mr. Fraser's name, as the discoverer, and first explorer of the golden stream which bears his name, will be remembered with honor long after most of his Provincial contemporaries have been forgotten.*

Twenty Years Later

Twenty years after Simon Fraser's 1808 journey to the sea, George Simpson, the Governor of the Hudson's Bay Company, followed the same route. Fraser had expected that Mackenzie had exaggerated the river's hazards, and Simpson had similar doubts about Fraser's reports. There had been no

exaggeration. Simpson stated that Simon Fraser's journey had been "an undertaking, compared to which...the much talked of and high sounding performances of His Majesty's recent discovery expeditions in the Arctic regions, were excursions of pleasure."

Hudson's Bay Company Governor George Simpson and his party descend the Fraser River in 1828.

For Discovery

1. In a group, prepare a presentation on the United Empire Loyalists. Include where they settled, when they came north from the United States, and what their lifestyle was like — occupations, recreation, social life, religion and so on.

2. You are transported back in time to the year 1808. You are one of the men Simon Fraser chooses to take on his journey of exploration. You can bring back only five things with you from the present. In order to convince Simon Fraser to take these things on the journey, prepare a chart showing how, where, when and why they will be useful. Remember, you already know what happened on the journey.

3. Prepare a time line of Simon Fraser's life. Begin in 1776 and end in 1862.

4. Research to find out about Lord Selkirk's Red River Settlement. Prepare a short essay on the settlement — its people, their way of life, how the settlement affected the Métis and the fur trade.

5. In a group, plan a trip to the northern wilderness of Canada. Let each member of your group provide a list of necessary supplies such as: food, clothing, camping gear, safety equipment, medical supplies, entertainment equipment, hunting and fishing gear. Compare lists and then prepare one which has the fewest but most efficient items.

6. In a short essay describe how the Natives were helpful to Simon Fraser in his explorations. Include transportation, clothing, hospitality, equipment and other things Fraser may have received or learned from the Natives.

Glossary

Bateaux   Flat-bottomed boats used to carry freight along the St. Lawrence and to ferry goods between sailing ships and the shore.

Cache   To store something in a hiding place for later use.

Canot du nord   The birchbark canoe fur traders usually used on the rivers and lakes of the Northwest. Smaller than the freight canoes used from Montreal and through the Great Lakes, it varied in size and might be up to ten metres long.

Delta   Flat area at the mouth of some rivers where the river divides into several branches.

Latitude   A measure of distance from the equator calculated in degrees. One degree of latitude represents just over 110 kilometres.

Nor'Westers   Name for the North West Company traders.

Pays d'en haut   Fur traders' name for the country north and west of Lake Superior.

Pemmican   Dried buffalo meat that had been pounded to separate the fibres and then mixed with melted fat. The result was a concentrated, very nutritious food that kept for months, even years.

Portage   Canoes and their cargo often had to be carried from one lake or river to another or around rapids and falls. A place where this happened was called a portage as was the act of doing it.

Voyageurs   The men, usually French Canadian or Métis, who paddled and steered the canoes of the inland fur trade.

Wintering partner   Those partners of the North West Company who spent the winters at the western trading posts.

Index